Learning to Swim

Contents

written by Pam Holden

You will have a teacher to help you find out how to swir

teacher

Your teacher will show you what to do.

You will have good things to help you.

You will walk and jump in the water.

You will find out how to blow bubbles in the water.

Your teacher will show you how to make a good kick.

bubbles

Next you will find out
how to float on your back.

You will find out how
to breathe in the water.

Then you will go for a little swim.

board

You will have a board to help you.

Next you will find out how to use your arms.

Then you will swim a little way.

swimming

Soon you will go
for a big swim.

backstroke

You will find out how to swim on your back.

Some day you will find out how to dive, too!